Malala Yousafzai
EDUCATION ACTIVIST

by Connor Stratton

Focus Readers
BEACON

www.focusreaders.com

Copyright © 2021 by Focus Readers®, Lake Elmo, MN 55042. All rights reserved. No part of this book may be reproduced or utilized in any form or by any means without written permission from the publisher.

Focus Readers is distributed by North Star Editions:
sales@northstareditions.com | 888-417-0195

Produced for Focus Readers by Red Line Editorial.

Photographs ©: Raphael Lafargue/Abaca/Sipa USA/AP Images, cover, 1; Kyodo/AP Images, 4; Rui Vieira/AP Images, 6; Shutterstock Images, 8, 14, 17, 20–21; Naveed Ali/AP Images, 11; Sherin Zada/AP Images, 13; Cornelius Poppe/NTB Scanpix/AP Images, 19; Charles Krupa/AP Images, 22, 29; Muhammed Muheisen/AP Images, 25; Nelson Antoine/AP Images, 26

Library of Congress Cataloging-in-Publication Data
Names: Stratton, Connor, author.
Title: Malala Yousafzai : education activist / by Connor Stratton.
Description: Lake Elmo, MN : Focus Readers, [2021] | Series: Important women | Includes index. | Audience: Grades 4-6
Identifiers: LCCN 2020037835 (print) | LCCN 2020037836 (ebook) | ISBN 9781644936948 (hardcover) | ISBN 9781644937303 (paperback) | ISBN 9781644938027 (pdf) | ISBN 9781644937662 (ebook)
Subjects: LCSH: Yousafzai, Malala, 1997---Juvenile literature. | Women social reformers--Pakistan--Biography--Juvenile literature. | Women political activists--Pakistan--Biography--Juvenile literature. | Girls--Education--Pakistan--Juvenile literature.
Classification: LCC LC2330 .S78 2021 (print) | LCC LC2330 (ebook) | DDC 371.822095491--dc23
LC record available at https://lccn.loc.gov/2020037835
LC ebook record available at https://lccn.loc.gov/2020037836

Printed in the United States of America
Mankato, MN
012021

About the Author

Connor Stratton writes and edits children's books. He loves poetry and history, especially by and about fierce women. Every day he works to be a better feminist. He lives in Minnesota.

Table of Contents

CHAPTER 1
Using Her Voice 5

CHAPTER 2
Becoming an Activist 9

CHAPTER 3
Nobel Peace Prize 15

TOPIC SPOTLIGHT
Girls' Education 20

CHAPTER 4
Lifting Up Others 23

Focus on Malala Yousafzai • 28
Glossary • 30
To Learn More • 31
Index • 32

Chapter 1

Using Her Voice

On July 12, 2013, Malala Yousafzai spoke to a crowd. Young leaders from 100 countries listened. She was at the United Nations (UN). The UN helps countries work together to solve problems.

Malala Yousafzai wore a shawl that had belonged to Benazir Bhutto, Pakistan's first female prime minister.

 Malala (second from right) learned the values of compassion and bravery from her family.

Malala spoke about education. She said countries should provide free school to all children. She said school was especially important for girls. Malala had worked for these beliefs for years. Her **activism** had put her in danger. But she continued to speak up.

Malala's background played a large role in her beliefs. She practiced Islam. She said this religion valued children's education. Malala was also **Pashtun**. She said her people believed in peace and education. Her speech told how these two ideas could change the world.

Did You Know?

Malala gave the speech to the UN on her 16th birthday.

Chapter 2

Becoming an Activist

Malala Yousafzai was born on July 12, 1997. She grew up in the Swat Valley of Pakistan. Her father worked as an activist. He started a school for girls. As a result, Malala always loved learning.

 Swat Valley is in northwestern Pakistan. The area is known for its beautiful mountains.

In 2007, a **militant** group took over Swat. This group was called Tehrik-e-Taliban Pakistan (TTP). TTP opposed Pakistan's government. It also opposed US military forces in the area.

TTP followed an **extreme** kind of Islam. For example, many TTP

Did You Know?

Malala is named after Malalai. She was a Pashtun hero who fought against the British in 1880.

 A student reads to her class at a school in Swat Valley.

members believed girls should not go to school. Malala and her father opposed the group. So, they spoke out against it.

In early 2009, TTP shut down all girls' schools in Swat Valley.

The group also blew up more than 100 schools. In May 2009, Pakistan's army started fighting TTP in Swat. The area became unsafe. Malala's family had to leave. They were **displaced** for months.

Malala continued to speak out against TTP. The group wanted her

Did You Know?

In 2009, Malala started writing a blog for a news website. She told what life was like under TTP control.

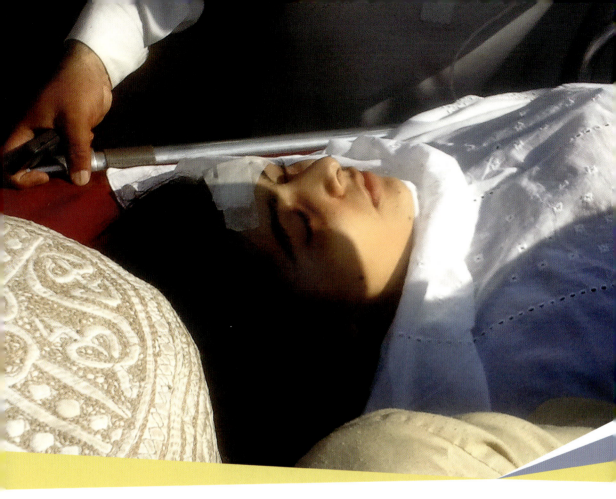

 Malala was shot in the head. The attack left her badly injured.

to stop. So, in October 2012, TTP members shot Malala. She nearly died. Her story spread around the world.

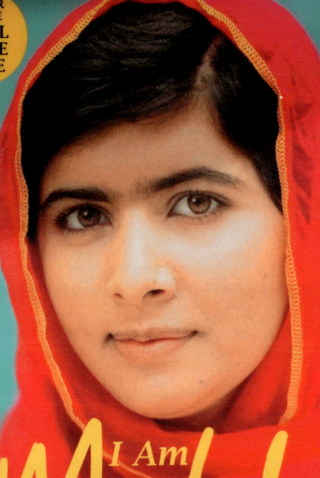

Chapter 3

Nobel Peace Prize

After the shooting, Malala was flown to England. She slowly got better. By March 2013, Malala was well enough for school. She stayed in England. She also wrote a book about her life.

People all over the world read Malala's book and learned about her story.

Malala continued her activism. In July 2013, she spoke at the UN in New York City. In October, she met with US president Barack Obama. Malala told him US **drone strikes** in Pakistan were wrong.

She also started the Malala Fund. The group helped provide education to girls. In early 2014,

Did You Know?

By 2016, Malala's book had sold more than 1.8 million copies.

 In June 2014, more than 80,000 people lived in the Zaatari refugee camp in Jordan.

Malala went to Jordan. She met with **refugees** from Syria. They were living in camps. The camps did not have buildings for schools.

So, people set up schools in tents. However, these schools did not always let in older girls. The Fund helped find women to teach those girls one-on-one. It also supported the tent schools.

In July 2014, Malala traveled to Kenya. She met with girls there. The girls told Malala their stories. They said they wanted to go to school. So, the Fund helped pay to build one. Malala even helped build it.

 Malala shared the Nobel Prize with Kailash Satyarthi. He also worked for children's rights.

In October 2014, Malala won the Nobel Peace Prize. At 17, she was the youngest person ever to receive this honor. But Malala was just getting started.

TOPIC SPOTLIGHT

Girls' Education

Many children around the world cannot attend school. For some, going to school costs too much. Conflict is another cause. Traveling to school may not be safe.

Many families make hard choices. They may have to choose which children receive education. Girls are much less likely than boys to get enough education. Some people believe girls' education is less important. Schools also may not be safe for girls.

However, many people are helping. Some groups try to reduce **poverty** and conflict. Others bring schooling to low-income areas.

Girls in India are often unable to finish all 12 years of school.

Chapter 4

Lifting Up Others

Malala Yousafzai's work with the Malala Fund continued to grow. The Fund focused on areas with conflict or poverty. By 2018, it was working in the Middle East, Asia, Africa, and South America.

Yousafzai travels around the world for her work as an education activist.

Yousafzai wanted to give more girls a chance to tell their stories. The Fund created a website. Girls wrote about their activism. Then those stories appeared on the site. Girls could share art and photos, too.

Yousafzai also helped to create another book. *We Are Displaced* came out in 2019. This book was not just an **autobiography**. It told stories of other girls who had been displaced. The book showed how

 Yousafzai (left) talks with a girl living in the Azraq refugee camp in Jordan in 2015.

Yousafzai was not unique. Millions of girls had similar experiences.

In 2020, a virus spread around the world. To stay safe, many people had to stay home. The Malala Fund said that 10 million girls could lose access to schooling.

 Yousafzai often speaks about the power of words to make change.

So, the Fund helped put lessons and education materials online. It also supported people who had made learning apps. These computer programs helped children continue their education at home. As the virus spread, many more people used these apps.

Yousafzai knew that providing schooling to all girls was tough. But she had already made a difference. And she planned to focus on girls' education for years to come.

Did You Know?
Yousafzai continued her own education, too. She finished college in 2020.

FOCUS ON
Malala Yousafzai

Write your answers on a separate piece of paper.

1. Write a sentence summarizing the work the Malala Fund does.

2. What is one issue that is important to you? How could you speak up about it?

3. When was Malala's family forced to leave their home in Swat Valley?
   - **A.** 2007
   - **B.** 2009
   - **C.** 2018

4. How would reducing poverty help students?
   - **A.** More kids might have enough money to attend school.
   - **B.** More kids might decide to stay home.
   - **C.** More teachers would not be paid.

5. What does **unique** mean in this book?

*The book showed how Yousafzai was not **unique**. Millions of girls had similar experiences.*

- **A.** able to read or write
- **B.** famous around the world
- **C.** different from everyone else

6. What does **conflict** mean in this book?

***Conflict** is another cause. Traveling to school may not be safe.*

- **A.** a way to travel to school
- **B.** an easy way to fix a problem
- **C.** a struggle often involving violence

Answer key on page 32.

Glossary

activism
Actions to make social or political changes.

autobiography
The story of a person's life written by that person.

displaced
Forced to leave home, usually because of war or other dangers.

drone strikes
Missile attacks by aircraft that soldiers control from a distance.

extreme
Very different from beliefs or ideas held by most people in a certain area.

militant
Tending to use military violence.

Pashtun
A people who live in northwestern Pakistan and southeastern Afghanistan.

poverty
Not having enough money or resources to live easily.

refugees
People forced to leave their country due to war or other dangers.

To Learn More

BOOKS

Kaminski, Leah. *Assalam-o-Alaikum, Pakistan.* Ann Arbor, MI: Cherry Lake Publishing, 2020.

London, Martha. *Malala Yousafzai.* Minneapolis: Abdo Publishing, 2020.

Schwartz, Heather E. *Malala Yousafzai: Heroic Education Activist.* Minneapolis: Lerner Publications, 2020.

NOTE TO EDUCATORS

Visit **www.focusreaders.com** to find lesson plans, activities, links, and other resources related to this title.

Index

D
displaced, 12, 24

E
education, 6–7, 16, 20, 26–27

I
Islam, 7, 10

M
Malala Fund, 16, 18, 23–26

N
Nobel Peace Prize, 19

P
Pakistan, 9–10, 12, 16
Pashtun, 7, 10
poverty, 20, 23

S
school, 6, 9, 11–12, 15, 17–18, 20, 25, 27
Swat Valley, 9–12

T
Tehrik-e-Taliban Pakistan (TTP), 10–13

U
United Nations (UN), 5, 7, 16

Answer Key: 1. Answers will vary; 2. Answers will vary; 3. B; 4. A; 5. C; 6. C